Now you
violin s
reco

TAKE
THE
LEAD

violin

International
MUSIC
Publications

International Music Publications Limited
Griffin House 161 Hammersmith Road London W6 8BS England

DON'T BE
A MUSIC
COPYCAT!

The copying of © copyright
material is a criminal offence
and may lead to prosecution.

Series Editor: Sadie Cook

Editorial, production and recording: Artemis Music Limited
Design and production: Space DPS Limited

Published 1999

International MUSIC Publications

IMP

International Music Publications Limited

England: Griffin House
                  161 Hammersmith Road
                  London W6 8BS

Germany: Marstallstr. 8
                  D-80539 München

Denmark: Danmusik
                  Vognmagergade 7
                  DK1120 Copenhagen K

Carisch

Italy: Via Campania 12
                  20098 San Giuliano Milanese
                  Milano

Spain: Magallanes 25
                  28015 Madrid

France: 20 Rue de la Ville-l'Eveque
                  75008 Paris

violin

TAKE THE LEAD

In the Book...

On the CD...

Demonstration

Backing

She Caught The Katy And Left Me A Mule To Ride

Words and Music by
Taj Mahal and Yank Rachel

Gimme Some Lovin'

Words and Music by Steve Winwood,
Muff Winwood and Spencer Davis

Demonstration

Backing

Everybody Needs Somebody To Love

Words and Music by Bert Berns,
Solomon Burke and Jerry Wexler

Demonstration

Backing

Shake A Tail Feather

Words and Music by Otis Hayes,
Andre Williams and Verlie Rice

The Old Landmark

Words and Music by Adeline M Brunner

Demonstration   Backing

Think

Words and Music by
Ted White and Aretha Franklin

Moderately

Demonstration   Backing

Minnie The Moocher

Words and Music by Cab Calloway,
Irving Mills and Clarence Gaskill

Sweet Home Chicago

Words and Music by Robert Johnson

Demonstration

Backing

10/99

Reproduced and printed by
Halstan & Co. Ltd., Amersham, Bucks., England

You can be the featured soloist with
TAKE THE LEAD

Collect these titles, each with demonstration and full backing tracks on CD.

90s Hits

The Air That I Breathe
(Simply Red)

Angels
(Robbie Williams)

How Do I Live
(LeAnn Rimes)

I Don't Want To Miss A Thing
(Aerosmith)

I'll Be There For You
(The Rembrandts)

My Heart Will Go On
(Celine Dion)

**Something About The Way
You Look Tonight**
(Elton John)

Frozen
(Madonna)

Order ref: 6725A – Flute

Order ref: 6726A – Clarinet

Order ref: 6727A – Alto Saxophone

Order ref: 6728A – Violin

Movie Hits

Because You Loved Me
(Up Close And Personal)

Blue Monday
(The Wedding Singer)

**(Everything I Do)
I Do It For You**
(Robin Hood: Prince Of Thieves)

I Don't Want To Miss A Thing
(Armageddon)

I Will Always Love You
(The Bodyguard)

Star Wars (Main Title)
(Star Wars)

The Wind Beneath My Wings
(Beaches)

You Can Leave Your Hat On
(The Full Monty)

Order ref: 6908A – Flute

Order ref: 6909A – Clarinet

Order ref: 6910A – Alto Saxophone

Order ref: 6911A –Tenor Saxophone

Order ref: 6912A – Violin

TV Themes

Coronation Street

**I'll Be There For You
(theme from Friends)**

Match Of The Day

(Meet) The Flintstones

Men Behaving Badly

Peak Practice

The Simpsons

The X-Files

Order ref: 7003A – Flute

Order ref: 7004A – Clarinet

Order ref: 7005A – Alto Saxophone

Order ref: 7006A – Violin

Christmas Songs

**The Christmas Song
(Chestnuts Roasting On An
Open Fire)**

Frosty The Snowman

**Have Yourself A Merry
Little Christmas**

Little Donkey

**Rudolph The Red-Nosed
Reindeer**

**Santa Claus Is Comin'
To Town**

Sleigh Ride

Winter Wonderland

Order ref: 7022A – Flute

Order ref: 7023A – Clarinet

Order ref: 7024A – Alto Saxophone

Order ref: 7025A – Violin

Order ref: 7026A – Piano

Order ref: 7027A – Drums

The Blues Brothers

**She Caught The Katy And
Left Me A Mule To Ride**

Gimme Some Lovin'

Shake A Tail Feather

**Everybody Needs Somebody
To Love**

The Old Landmark

Think

Minnie The Moocher

Sweet Home Chicago

Order ref: 7079A - Flute

Order ref: 7080A - Clarinet

Order ref: 7081A - Alto Saxophone

Order ref: 7082A - Tenor Saxophone

Order ref: 7083A - Trumpet

Order ref: 7084A - Violin